SIMPLISSIME

Disney

THE SIMPLE FAMILY COOKBOOK

SIMPLISSIME

J.-F. Mallet

THE SIMPLE FAMILY COOKBOOK

ilex

This book is the fruit of times spent in the kitchen with my two daughters, Jeanne and Paula. Ever since they were small children, they have been giving me ideas for easy recipes, and for this book they had fun inventing recipes to suit the Disney heroes and heroines who are much more familiar to them than to me. We regularly cook together as a family; it is a fun way to get them to eat everything, even spinach, broccoli and turnips...

In addition to these wonderful shared moments, it is a way for me to make them aware of the taste of 'real' food, introduce them to new ingredients and, above all, to prepare balanced dishes for them without too much sugar and fat. As far as possible I avoid ready-made products stuffed with hidden sugars, fats, colourings, preservatives and other dubious substances whose impact on health is not fully known.

This does not mean that they are not occasionally allowed to treat themselves to a cheese gratin or a nice homemade burger. I actually try to dismiss generally accepted ideas, because a homemade burger with grilled vegetables and good-quality meat is a balanced dish. For desserts, I do not overdo the sugar or butter, but we do know how to make food we enjoy.

In this book you will find 100 recipes, all in the style of children's favourite characters and all extremely easy to make using a variety of easily obtainable ingredients.

I hope you share some wonderful moments, both in the kitchen and at the table.

HOW TO USE THIS BOOK

In this book I am assuming that at home you have:

- Running water
- A cooker
- A refrigerator
- A blender
- A frying pan
- A cast-iron casserole dish
- A knife (very sharp)
- A pair of scissors
- Salt and pepper
- Oil

(If this is not the case, maybe now is the time to invest!)

What are the must-have ingredients?

Fruits and vegetables: Use fresh and preferably in season, but don't hesitate to fall back on the raw frozen version. I would advise you to buy organic; after all, this is better for your children's heath, especially when you use the zest of citrus fruits and the skins of fruits and vegetables. Do not hesitate to use different varieties of vegetables.

Herbs: You can't beat fresh herbs, so try to use them where you can! If all else fails, you can always use the frozen or dried versions (with the exception of oregano as it is not as good).

Oils: I prefer olive oil – always extra-virgin, which is the best for your health. For the occasional variation, a drizzle of sesame oil or walnut oil can brighten up a dish and change the seasoning of a salad.

Spices: Paprika, curry powder, cumin and turmeric feature frequently in my dishes. Spices enable you to invent new flavours, add a little touch of the exotic and, most importantly, to cut down on salt. All the recipes tell you to season with salt and pepper, but I recommend using salt in moderation, because too much salt is bad for your health.

Tinned goods: Stock up on tins of tuna and sardines in oil, coconut milk and the indispensable tomato purée or chopped tomatoes. That's all...

Condiments: I always have mustard, pesto and balsamic vinegar in my larder; they can rescue your dinner in an instant.

Which techniques should you use?

Cooking pasta: Cook in a large saucepan in plenty of boiling salted water. Pay attention to the cooking time if you like your pasta *al dente*.

Marinating: Soak an ingredient in an aromatic mixture to flavour or tenderise it.

Beating egg whites until stiff: Add a pinch of salt to the egg whites and use an electric whisk, gradually increasing the speed. Always beat the whites in the same direction to prevent them from going grainy.

Zesting citrus fruit: There are two ways of zesting citrus fruit. For beginners – and to get a very fine zest – use a cheese grater on the peel of the fruit, going over each area just once, without touching the white pith. For professionals – and to get zest that looks like vermicelli – use a zester.

What equipment should you choose?

Hand blender: Also known as a stick blender, this is used to mix liquids (soups, smoothies, milkshakes, etc.). It is very handy, inexpensive and space-saving, and also means less washing-up, because you use it directly in whatever you are mixing, with no need to transfer it to a bowl.

Blender: Used for making juices.

Which oven temperature?

140°C: Gas mark 1	160°C: Gas mark 3	190°C: Gas mark 5	220°C: Gas mark 7
150°C: Gas mark 2	180°C: Gas mark 4	200°C: Gas mark 6	230°C: Gas mark 8

That's everything. All you have to do now is follow the recipe!

COCKTAIL BRIOCHE FOR THE BALL

Brioche loaf
1 (large)

Cream cheese
360g

Cucumber
½

Tuna in brine
1 tin (130g drained)

Mint
1 bunch

: 6

Preparation: 15 mins

• Mix the drained **tuna** with the **cream cheese**. Cut the **brioche** horizontally into 6 slices. Wash the **cucumber** and slice thinly. Wash the **mint** and pick off the leaves.

• Spread each slice of **brioche** with the tuna and **cream cheese** mixture, add the sliced **cucumber** and the **mint** leaves and then put the **brioche** back together.

RILLETTES IN A SARDINE TIN

Cream cheese
180g

Sardines in olive oil
2 tins

Limes
x 2

 **Salt, pepper**

 : 6

⏱
Preparation: 10 mins

• Drain the **sardines** and crush them with the **cream cheese** and the zest and juice of the **limes**. Season with salt and pepper.

• Serve the rillettes in the sardine tin and enjoy.

COCKTAIL BLINIS

Crème fraîche
120g

Chives
1 large or 2 small bunches

Smoked salmon
2 small slices

Blinis
8

 Salt, pepper

 : 4

🕐

Preparation: 10 mins

• Cut the **smoked salmon** into thin strips.

• Cut up the **chives** with scissors, saving a few for decoration, and mix with the **crème fraîche**. Season with salt and pepper.

• When it is time to serve, spread the **petit-suisse** mixture on the **blinis**, top with the **salmon** strips and enjoy.

JUDY HOPPS' CARROTS WITH ORANGE

Small carrots with tops	Greek yogurt
1 bunch	250g

Orange	Coriander
1	1 bunch

  Salt, pepper

 **: 4**

Preparation: 5 mins

- Trim and wash the **carrots**. Cut the largest ones in half.
- Chop up the **coriander** and mix with the **yogurt** and the zest and juice of the **orange**. Season with salt and pepper.
- Eat the **carrots** with the dip.

MULAN'S CRISPY CRACKERS

Taramasalata
1 small pot (100g)

Prawn crackers
12

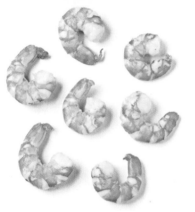

Prawns
6 (cooked and peeled)

Mint
12 leaves

 : 4

Preparation: 5 mins

• Just before serving (so the crackers do not go soft), place a little **taramasalata**, 1 **mint** leaf and ½ **prawn** on each **cracker**.

16

BEAUTY'S BOUQUET OF ROSES

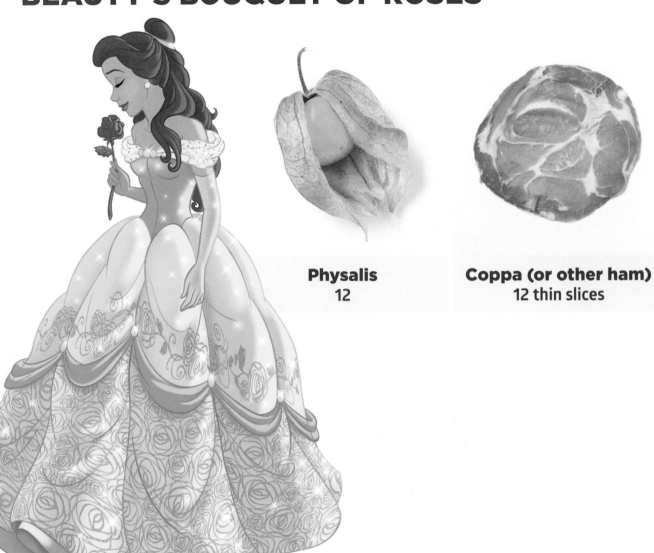

Physalis
12

Coppa (or other ham)
12 thin slices

 : 4

⏱

Preparation: 5 mins

- Carefully peel back the **physalis** leaves.
- Wrap each fruit in 1 slice of **coppa**.
- Arrange on a dish and enjoy.

PONGO'S NIBBLES

Pizza dough
1 rectangle

Minced beef
200g (5% fat)

Mustard
2 tablespoons

Grated Parmesan
4 tablespoons

 Salt, pepper

 : 4

Preparation: 10 mins
Refrigeration: 30 mins
Cooking time: 15 mins

- Preheat the oven to 200°C.
- Mix together the **minced beef**, **mustard** and half the **Parmesan**. Season with salt and pepper.
- Spread the mince over the **pizza dough**. Roll the sides towards the centre and chill in the fridge.
- Cut the roll into slices. Arrange on a baking sheet lined with baking paper. Sprinkle with the remaining **Parmesan** and bake for 15 mins.

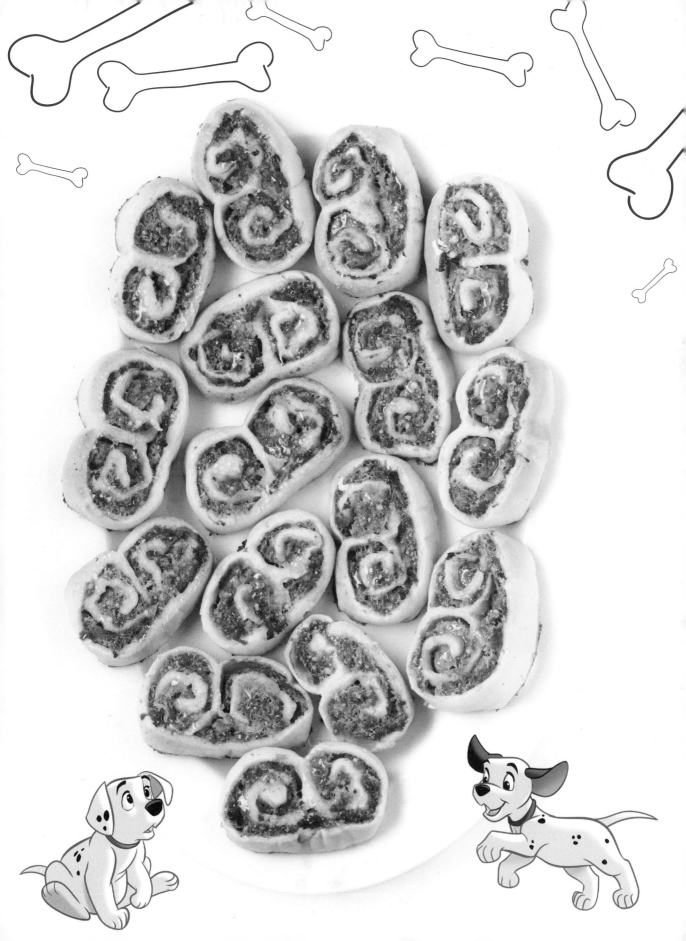

HUMMUS WITH CUMIN

Chickpeas
1 tin (530g drained)

Olive oil
6 tablespoons

Garlic
2 cloves

Lemons
2

Cumin seeds
1 teaspoon

  Salt, pepper

 : 4

Preparation: 10 mins

- Drain and rinse the **chickpeas**. Heat in a saucepan with 50ml water.
- Mix the **chickpeas** with the cooking water, 5 tablespoons of **olive oil**, the chopped **garlic**, the juice of the **lemons** and half the **cumin**. Season with salt and pepper and leave to cool.
- Transfer to a serving dish and drizzle with the remaining **oil** and **cumin seeds**.

MULAN'S SPRING ROLLS

Spring roll wrappers	Cucumber
8 (large)	½

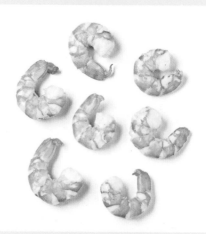

Cooked ham	Mint	Prawns
4 slices	2 bunches	16 (cooked and peeled)

 : 4

Preparation: 15 mins

• Moisten the **wrappers** under cold running water. Top with **prawns** cut in half, slices of **ham** cut in half, **cucumber** cut in sticks and **mint** leaves.

• Turn in the edges, roll up tightly and enjoy.

ABUELITA'S GUACAMOLE

Avocados 2	Smoked salmon 4 small slices

Limes 2	Ground cumin 1 teaspoon	Coriander 1 bunch

 **Salt, pepper**

 : 4

⊘
Preparation: 5 mins

• Peel the **avocados**, remove the stones and mix the flesh with the juice of the **limes** and the **cumin**. Season with salt and pepper.

• Arrange the **guacamole** on a dish and add the **smoked salmon** cut into pieces.

• Sprinkle with **coriander** leaves and enjoy.

HAWAIIAN SALAD

Pineapple
1 (small)

Rice
80g

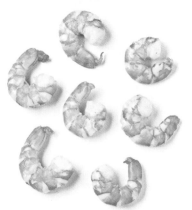

Prawns
100g (cooked and peeled)

Olive oil
2 tablespoons

Cooked ham
2 slices

 Salt, pepper

🐭 : 4

⏱
Preparation: 10 mins
Cooking time: 10 mins

- Cook the **rice** in boiling salted water and leave to cool.
- Cut the **pineapple** in half lengthways, scoop out the flesh and cut into small pieces. Chop the **ham** and mix it with the **pineapple**, **rice**, **prawns** and **olive oil**. Season with salt and pepper.
- Arrange the salad in the **pineapple** shells and enjoy.

28

TROPICAL-STYLE FISH

Salmon steaks
4 (skinless)

Coconut milk
250ml

Limes
4

Coriander
2 bunches (chopped)

Cucumber
¼

Salt, pepper

: 4

Preparation: 5 mins
Marination: 30 mins

• Cut the **salmon steaks** into cubes and mix with the juice of the **limes**, the sliced **cucumber**, the **coconut milk** and the **coriander**.

• Season with salt and pepper. Marinate for 30 mins in the refrigerator and serve.

MICKEY AND FRIENDS' SALAD

Sweetcorn
1 small tin (200g)

Roma tomatoes
4

Paprika
2 tablespoons

Avocado
1

Lemons
2

 **Salt, pepper**

Olive oil

: 4

Preparation: 10 mins

• Cut the **tomatoes** in half and deseed.
• Chop the **avocado** into small pieces, mix with the **sweetcorn** and spoon into the **tomatoes**.
• Mix the **paprika** with the juice of the **lemons** and 3 tablespoons of olive oil. Season with salt and pepper, pour over the **tomatoes** and serve.

SUMMER RATATOUILLE

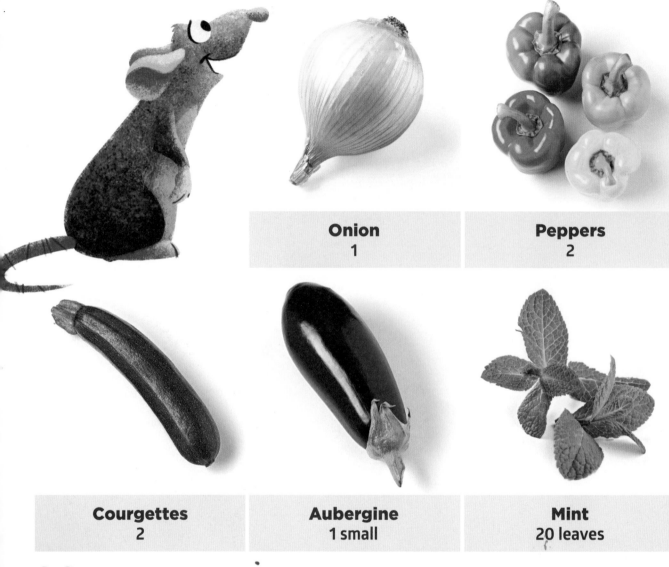

Onion 1	Peppers 2
Courgettes 2	**Aubergine** 1 small

Mint
20 leaves

 Salt, pepper

Olive oil

 : 4

Preparation: 25 mins
Cooking time: 45 mins

• Chop the **onion**, **peppers**, **courgettes** and **aubergine** into small pieces.

• Heat 6 tablespoons of olive oil and sauté the vegetables without browning. Season with salt and pepper and simmer for 45 mins over a low heat.

• Leave to cool, add the **mint**, chopped with scissors, and serve.

THE EMPEROR'S CEVICHE

Cucumber
1

Cod fillets
2

Limes
4

Coconut milk
200ml

Coriander
2 tablespoons (chopped)

 Salt, pepper

 Olive oil

 : 4

🕐
Preparation: 5 mins
Marination: 10 mins

- Cut the **cucumber** in half lengthways and scoop out the flesh. Cut into 8 boats.
- Cut the **cod** into pieces and mix with the **cucumber** flesh, **coconut milk**, the juice of the **limes**, 2 tablespoons of olive oil and **coriander**.
- Marinate for 10 mins and arrange in the **cucumber** boats. Season with salt and pepper and serve.

NANI'S SALAD

Romaine lettuces
2

Mixed seafood
400g (frozen)

Blueberries
1 punnet

Olive oil
6 tablespoons

Soy sauce
4 tablespoons

 Pepper

 : 4

⏱
Preparation: 10 mins
Cooking time: 5 mins

• Cut the **lettuces** in half lengthways, remove and chop a little of the hearts.

• Sauté the **seafood** for 5 mins in a pan with the **olive oil** and **soy sauce**. Leave to cool, then mix with the **blueberries** and chopped **lettuce**.

• Arrange in the **lettuces**, pour over the cooking juices, season with pepper and serve.

PACHA'S SALAD

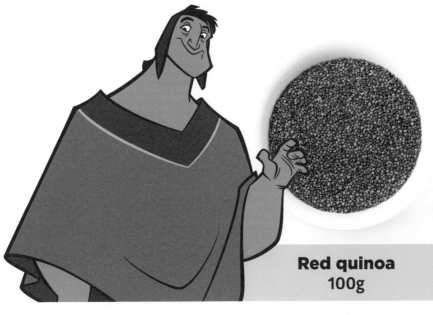

Red quinoa 100g	**Passion fruits** 4

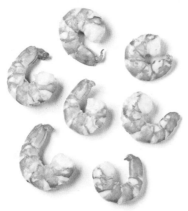

Prawns 16 (cooked and peeled)	**Coriander** 1 bunch (chopped)

 Salt, pepper

 Olive oil

 : 4

Preparation: 5 mins
Cooking time: 10 mins
Resting time: 10 mins

40

• Cook the **quinoa** for 10 mins in 200ml water with the lid on. Turn off the heat and leave to swell for 10 mins.

• Cut the **passion fruits** in half. Scoop out the flesh and mix with the cold **quinoa**, **coriander** and chopped **prawns**. Season.

• Fill the **passion fruit** shells with the mixture and drizzle with olive oil.

DUCHESS'S LIGHT SUPPER

Tuna in brine
2 tins (260g in total)

Rocket
150g

Eggs
5

    Salt, pepper

Butter (for greasing)

: 4

Preparation: 5 mins
Cooking time: 30 mins

• Preheat the oven to 180°C.

• Drain the **tuna**, mix with the beaten **eggs** and 100g of the **rocket**, chopped finely with scissors, and season with salt and pepper.

• Transfer to a greased cake tin and bake for 30 mins.

• Serve cold in thick slices with the remainder of the **rocket**.

DUMBO'S FAVOURITE SALAD

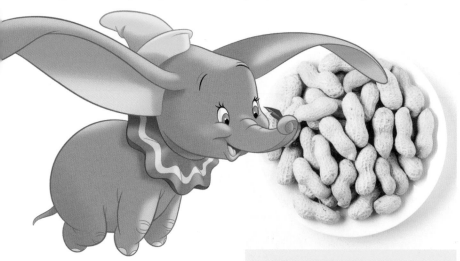

Unshelled peanuts
100g

Grated carrot
250g

Coriander
2 bunches

Soy sauce
3 tablespoons

Lemongrass
2 stalks

 Salt, pepper

 **Groundnut oil**

: 4

Preparation: 10 mins

• Shell the **peanuts**. Slice the **lemongrass**. Wash the **coriander** and chop roughly.
• When you are about to eat, mix all the ingredients together in a salad bowl, season with salt and pepper, drizzle with oil and serve.

AUTUMN SALAD

Oak leaf lettuce
1

Walnuts
25 halves

Black grapes
2 bunches

Walnut oil
2 tablespoons

Balsamic vinegar
2 tablespoons

 Salt, pepper

🐭 : 4

⏱
Preparation: 5 mins

• Wash the **grapes** and cut in half. Roughly crush the **walnut** halves. Wash the **lettuce** and pick off the leaves.

• When you are about to eat, mix all the ingredients together in a salad bowl, season with salt and pepper and serve.

SWEETCORN PANCAKES

Romaine lettuce
1

Sweetcorn
1 medium tin (325g)

Plain flour
2 tablespoons

Eggs
2

Grated Parmesan
4 tablespoons

 Salt, pepper

 Oil

 : 4

Preparation: 15 mins
Cooking time: 10 mins

• Blend the **sweetcorn** with the **eggs** and **flour**. Season with salt and pepper. Heat 3 tablespoons of oil in a large frying pan and add tablespoons of batter to form small pancakes. Cook for 1 min on each side.

• Chop the **lettuce** and mix with 1 tablespoon of oil and the **Parmesan**. Season with salt and pepper, add the warm pancakes and serve.

MINNIE'S GREEN SALAD

French beans
200g

Courgettes
2

Garden peas
200g (fresh or frozen)

Little Gem lettuces
2

Mint
20 leaves

 Salt, pepper

 **Olive oil**

 **: 4**

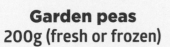
Preparation: 15 mins
Cooking time: 10 mins

- Cook the **French beans**, the sliced **courgettes** and the **peas** for 10 mins in boiling salted water. Drain and rinse in cold water.
- Separate the **lettuce** leaves and mix with the vegetables and **mint**.
- Season with salt and pepper and a drizzle of olive oil and serve.

MUSHU'S SALAD

Chicken breasts
2

Sesame oil
4 tablespoons

Sesame seeds
4 tablespoons

Coriander
1 bunch

Bean sprouts
200g

 Salt, pepper

: 4

Preparation: 5 mins
Cooking time: 5 mins

• Roughly chop the **coriander** and arrange on a dish with the **bean sprouts**.

• Chop the **chicken breasts** and sauté over a high heat with the **oil** and **sesame seeds**. Season with salt and pepper.

• Arrange on the dish with the cooking juices and serve immediately.

MOUNT OLYMPUS TOMATOES

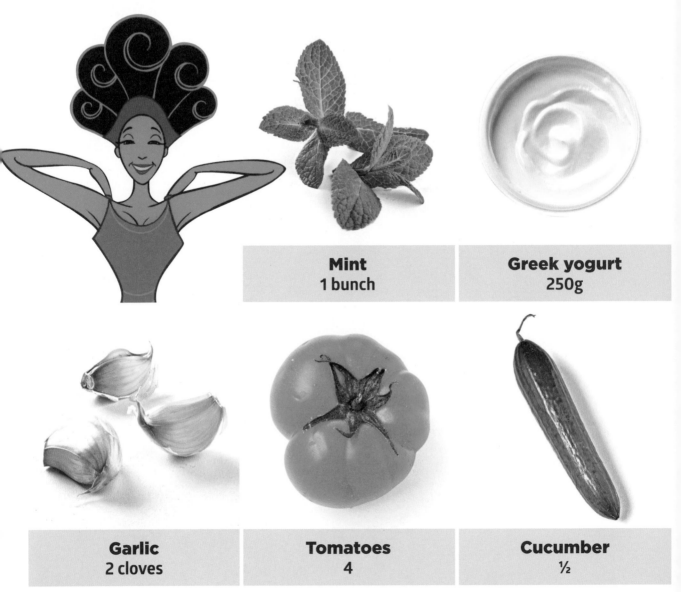

Mint	Greek yogurt
1 bunch	250g

Garlic	Tomatoes	Cucumber
2 cloves	4	½

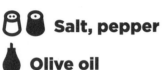 Salt, pepper

Olive oil

 : 4

Preparation: 10 mins

• Chop the **mint**, setting a few leaves aside. Peel the **garlic**. Grate the **cucumber** and **garlic** and mix with the **mint** and **yogurt**.

• Cut the **tomatoes** in half, deseed and top with the sauce. Season with salt and pepper.

• Add the remaining **mint** leaves and serve with a drizzle of olive oil.

MR SMEE'S SOUP

Watermelon ½ (small)	Courgettes 2

Mint
1 bunch

 Salt, pepper

 Olive oil

 : 4

Preparation: 10 mins
Cooking time: 20 mins

• Chop up **courgettes** and cook for 20 mins over a low heat in 400ml water. Leave to cool. Blend the soup with three-quarters of the **mint**, using a hand blender. Season with salt and pepper.

• Scoop the flesh out of the **watermelon** and cut into pieces. Pour the soup into the **melon** shell and add the flesh and the remaining **mint**. Serve with a drizzle of olive oil.

VITAMIN-RICH GAZPACHO

Tomatoes
4

Cucumber
½

Basil
1 bunch

Kiwis
2

 Salt, pepper

 : 4

🕐
Preparation: 5 mins

• Cut the **cucumber**, **tomatoes** and **kiwis** into small pieces, but set aside four slices of **kiwi**.
• Put everything in a blender, add the **basil** leaves and 200ml of water. Season with salt and pepper and blend.
• Spoon into bowls. Place one slice of **kiwi** on each bowl and serve.

RÉMY'S FAMOUS SOUP

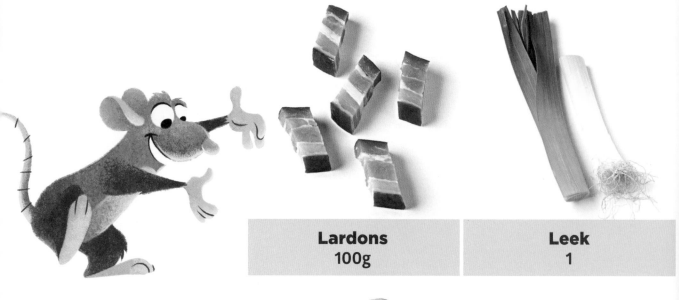

Lardons 100g	Leek 1

Turnips 2	Carrots 4

  Salt, pepper

🐭 : 4

⏱
Preparation: 5 mins
Cooking time: 35 mins

• Peel the **leek**, **turnips** and **carrots**, chop into small pieces and place in a lidded pan with the **lardons** and 1 litre of water.

• Bring to the boil, then simmer for 30 mins over a low heat. Add a little more water if too much has evaporated.

• Season with salt and pepper and serve.

SOUP OF THE FOREST

Cranberries
2 tablespoons

Oyster mushrooms
200g

Blueberries
1 punnet (125g)

Chanterelles
200g

Lardons
200g

 Salt, pepper

🐭 : 4

⏱
Preparation: 10 mins
Cooking time: 20 mins

- Wash the **mushrooms** and remove the stalks.
- Sauté the **lardons** for 1 min over a high heat in a dry pan. Add all the **mushrooms** and brown for 5 mins, stirring continuously. Add the **blueberries**, **cranberries** and 700ml water.
- Season with salt and pepper and simmer for 15 mins over a low heat before serving.

FAIRY GODMOTHER'S MAGIC SOUP

Pumpkin
1 (approx 1.6kg)

Wholemeal bread
4 large slices

Grated Cheddar
180g

Salt, pepper

: 4–6

Preparation: 20 mins
Cooking time: 45 mins

• Preheat the oven to 180°C.
• Cut a hat off the **pumpkin**. Scoop out the flesh and cut into pieces. Cook for 15 mins, just covered with water, then blend. Halve the slices of **bread**.
• Fill the **pumpkin** with alternate layers of soup, **bread** and **Cheddar**, seasoning each layer with salt and pepper. Bake in the oven for 30 mins and serve.

THE FLASH BURGER

Burger buns
4 (cut in half)

Courgettes
3

Minced beef
400g (5% fat)

Aubergines
2

Tomatoes
6

  Salt, pepper

Oil

 : 4

Preparation: 15 mins
Cooking time: 50 mins

- Preheat the oven to 200°C.
- Slice the **vegetables** thinly and bake for 35 mins on a baking sheet with 2 tablespoons of oil. Season with salt and pepper.
- Meanwhile, shape the **minced beef** into four patties, season them, and fry in one tablespoon of oil over a medium heat until cooked through, turning once. Assemble and serve hot.

JOHN SMITH'S CORN ON THE COB

Corn on the cobs
4

Paprika
1 tablespoon

Curry powder
1 tablespoon

Dried oregano
1 tablespoon

Feta
70g

  Salt, pepper

 : 4

🕐

Preparation: 5 mins
Cooking time: 15 mins

• Cook the **corn cobs** for 15 mins in boiling water or steam.

• Sprinkle the corn with **curry powder**, **paprika** and **oregano** while still hot.

• Sprinkle with crumbled **feta**. Season with salt and pepper and serve.

TURKEY NUGGETS

| Turkey escalopes 4 | Eggs 2 |

| Cornflakes 150g | Greek yogurt 250g | Curry powder 3 tablespoons |

 Salt, pepper

 : 4

🕐

Preparation: 15 mins
Cooking time: 15 mins

- Preheat the oven to 180°C.
- Crush the **cornflakes**. Beat the **eggs**.
- Cut the **escalopes** in strips, dip them in the **egg** and then in the **cornflakes**. Arrange on a baking sheet lined with baking paper. Season with salt and pepper and bake for 15 mins.
- Mix the **yogurt** with the **curry powder** and serve with the nuggets.

SWEET POTATO OVEN CHIPS

Sweet potatoes
2

Red pepper
1

Tomatoes
3

Honey
2 tablespoons

Paprika
2 tablespoons

 Salt, pepper

 Oil

 : 4

Preparation: 10 mins
Cooking time: 40 mins

• Preheat the oven to 180°C.

• Peel the **sweet potatoes** and cut into chips. Arrange on a baking sheet with 2 tablespoons of oil. Season and bake for 20 mins.

• Chop the **pepper** and **tomatoes** and sauté in a saucepan with the **honey** and **paprika**, then reduce the heat and cook for 20 mins. Season, blend and serve with the chips.

POTATO WEDGES WITH CHIVE SAUCE

Chives
1 bunch

New red potatoes
800g

Paprika
2 tablespoons

Oil
2 tablespoons

Greek yogurt
500g

  Salt, pepper

 : 4

Preparation: 5 mins
Cooking time: 45 mins

- Preheat the oven to 180°C.
- Wash the **potatoes**, cut into wedges, and mix in a large bowl with the **oil** and **paprika**. Season with salt and pepper.
- Bake for 45 mins on a baking sheet lined with baking paper.
- Beat the **yogurt** with the chopped **chives** and serve with the **potato wedges**.

MIGUEL'S FAVOURITE EMPANADA

Shortcrust pastry
1 sheet

Minced beef
250g (5% fat)

Mozzarella
2 balls (chopped)

Ground cumin
2 tablespoons

 Salt, pepper

 : 2

Preparation: 10 mins
Cooking time: 30 mins

• Preheat the oven to 200°C.
• Unroll the **pastry** on its baking paper or on a baking sheet. Brown the **minced beef** then mix with the **cumin** and the **mozzarella**. Season with salt and pepper.
• Spread the mixture over half the **pastry**. Fold it over and press the edges together with a fork. Bake for 25 mins.

PIZZA PLANET SPECIAL

Pizza base
1

Minced beef
300g (5% fat)

Tomato sauce
4 tablespoons

Dried oregano
2 tablespoons

Mozzarella
1 ball

  Salt, pepper

Oil

 : 4

Preparation: 5 mins
Cooking time: approx
20 mins

• Preheat the oven to 200°C.
• Cut the **mozzarella** into big chunks. Form the **mince** into 8 balls and brown in a pan with oil. Place the **pizza base** on a baking sheet. Spread the **tomato sauce** over the surface of the **pizza base**. Add the **mozzarella** and the meatballs. Sprinkle with **oregano** and season.
• Bake until the base is crisp and serve.

HAWAIIAN PIZZA

Pizza base
1

Tomato sauce
4 tablespoons

Pineapple in syrup
4 slices

Cooked ham
2 slices

Grated Parmesan
2 tablespoons

 Salt, pepper

 : 4

Preparation: 5 mins
Cooking time: 25 mins

• Place the **pizza base** on a baking sheet lined with baking paper. Spread the **tomato sauce** over the entire **pizza base**.

• Add the **ham** into pieces and the slices of **pineapple**. Sprinkle with **Parmesan**. Season with salt and pepper.

• Bake in the oven for 25 mins and serve.

VEGGIE PIZZA WITH CHEESE

Pizza base
1 rectangle

Tomatoes
3

Courgette
1 (large)

Green pepper
1

Grated Cheddar
100g

 **Salt, pepper**

 : 4–6

Preparation: 10 mins
Cooking time: 35 mins

- Preheat the oven to 200°C.
- Place the **pizza base** on a baking sheet lined with baking paper.
- Slice the **vegetables** thinly, distribute over the **pizza base**, and season with salt and pepper. Sprinkle with the **Cheddar** and bake in the oven for 35 mins.
- Serve hot or cold.

GEPPETTO'S TORTELLINI

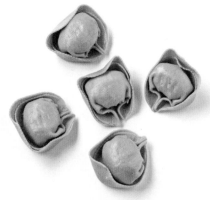

Tortellini
250g (spinach and ricotta)

Coppa (or other ham)
4 slices

Basil
1 bunch

Pine nuts
6 tablespoons

     Salt, pepper

Olive oil

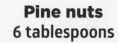 : 4

Preparation: 5 mins
Cooking time: 10 mins

• Cook the **tortellini** according to the package instructions in boiling water, then drain.

• Brown the **pine nuts** in a frying pan for 30 seconds, add the **tortellini** and the **coppa** and cook for 1 min, stirring continuously.

• Turn off the heat, add the **basil** and season with salt and pepper. Mix and serve with a drizzle of olive oil.

84

TONY'S SPAGHETTI

Spaghetti 300g	**Sausage meat** 400g

Tomato passata 500g	**Bouquets garnis** 2	**Onion** 1 large

 Salt, pepper

 Oil

 : 4

Preparation: 10 mins
Cooking time: 40 mins

- Form the **meat** into 12 balls. Chop the **onion**.
- Sauté the **meatballs** and **onion** in a frying pan with 1 tablespoon of oil for 5 mins over a high heat. Add the **tomato passata** and the **bouquets garnis** and season. Reduce the heat and simmer for a further 25 mins over a low heat.
- Serve with the **spaghetti** cooked *al dente*.

AUNT CASS'S SOBA

Buckwheat noodles
150g

Garden peas
200g (fresh or frozen)

Sesame oil
4 tablespoons

Sesame seeds
6 tablespoons

Eggs
4

 **Salt, pepper**

 : 4

Preparation: 10 mins
Cooking time: 10 mins

• Boil the **eggs** for exactly 5 mins then drain, cool and peel carefully.

• Plunge the **noodles** and the **peas** in boiling salted water for 5 mins. Drain and mix with the **sesame seeds** and **oil**. Season with salt and pepper.

• Serve with the halved **eggs**.

THE ARISTOCATS' SPAGHETTI

Spaghetti
300g

Sardines in oil
2 tins

Breakfast rusks
4

Rocket
60g

Dried garlic
1 teaspoon

 Salt

 : 4

Ⓒ
Preparation: 5 mins
Cooking time: 10 mins

• Cook the **spaghetti** *al dente* in boiling salted water. Drain and transfer to a frying pan with 1 tablespoon of the cooking water, the **sardines** cut into pieces plus the oil from one tin, the roughly crumbled **rusks** and the **dried garlic**. Mix and cook for 2 mins, stirring continuously.

• Remove from the heat, add the **rocket** and mix. Season with pepper and serve immediately.

LADY'S PASTA

Spaghetti 300g	Minced beef 400g (5% fat)

Basil 20 leaves	Cherry tomatoes 250g	Onion 1

  Salt, pepper

 Olive oil

 Grated Parmesan

 : 4

Preparation: 10 mins
Cooking time: 45 mins

- Heat some oil in a casserole dish and lightly brown the sliced **onion** and **minced beef**.
- Add the halved **tomatoes** and 500ml water and cook for 30 mins over a low heat.
- Cook the **spaghetti** in boiling salted water according to the package instructions and drain.
- Add the **spaghetti** and **basil** to the sauce, cook for 5 mins, then serve with **Parmesan**.

OMELETTE FOR LINGUINI

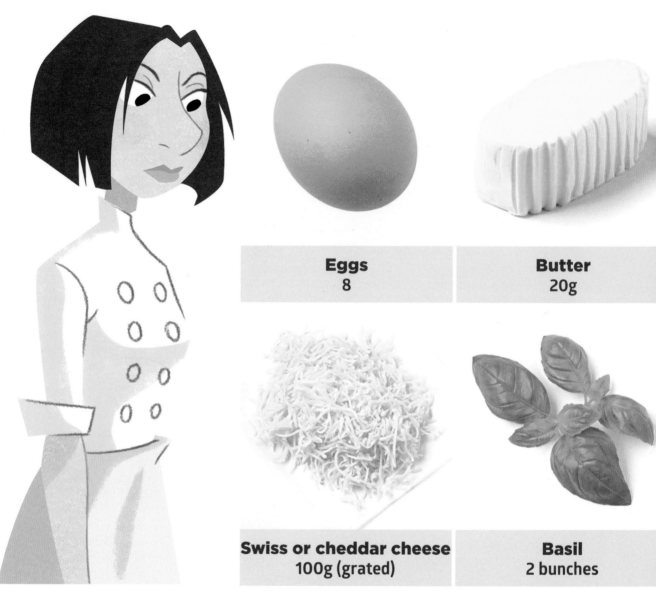

Eggs 8	Butter 20g
Swiss or cheddar cheese 100g (grated)	Basil 2 bunches

  Salt, pepper

Oil

 : 4

⏲

Preparation: 5 mins
Cooking time: 5 mins

• Beat the **eggs** with a fork, add the **basil** leaves chopped with scissors and the grated **cheese**. Season with salt and pepper.

• Melt the **butter** in a frying pan with 1 tablespoon of oil and pour in the egg mixture

• Cook for 4–5 mins, stirring regularly, until the **eggs** are completely cooked. Transfer the omelette to a dish and serve immediately.

STUFFED MUSHROOMS

Mushrooms
8 (large)

Dried oregano
1 tablespoon

Cream cheese
150g

  Salt, pepper

 Olive oil

 : 4

Preparation: 15 mins
Cooking time: 25 mins

• Preheat the oven to 180°C.

• Wash the **mushrooms**. Cut off and chop the stalks and mix with the **cream cheese** and **oregano**. Season with salt and pepper. Stuff the **mushrooms** with this mixture.

• Place the **mushrooms** in an ovenproof dish and bake for 25 mins. Serve with a drizzle of olive oil.

AUBERGINES STUFFED WITH RATATOUILLE

Aubergines 2	**Herbes de Provence** 1 tablespoon

Grated Cheddar 100g	**Tomatoes** 4	**Courgette** 1

  Salt, pepper

 : 4

🕐

Preparation: 15 mins
Cooking time: 45 mins

- Preheat the oven to 200°C.
- Halve the **aubergines** and scoop out the flesh.
- Dice the **aubergine** flesh, **tomatoes** and **courgette**. Mix with the **herbes de Provence**, season with salt and pepper and spoon into the **aubergine** shells.
- Place in an ovenproof dish with 600ml of water.
- Sprinkle with the **cheese** and bake for 45 mins.

HIRO'S FAVOURITE YAKITORIS

Chicken breasts
3

Sesame seeds
2 tablespoons

Shiitake mushrooms
10

Soy sauce
100ml

 Salt, pepper

 : 4

🕐
Preparation: 10 mins
Cooking time: 10 mins
Marination: 20 mins

- Preheat the oven to 180°C.
- Cut the **mushrooms** and **chicken** into small pieces. Assemble 12 skewers with alternate pieces of **chicken** and **mushroom**. Place in an ovenproof dish. Add the **sesame seeds** and **soy sauce** and marinate for 20 mins.
- Bake in the oven for 10 mins and serve with the cooking juices.

HECTOR'S CHORIZO FRY-UP

Baby corn
380g

Whole chorizo sausage
½

Cherry tomatoes
20

Coriander
1 bunch

 Salt, pepper

 : 4

Preparation: 6 mins
Cooking time: 6 mins

- Sauté the **baby corn** and the sliced **chorizo** for 5 mins over a high heat.
- Add the **cherry tomatoes**. Season with salt and pepper and cook for a further min.
- Serve immediately with the **coriander** leaves.

RATATOUILLE GUSTEAU-STYLE

Basil
1 bunch

Tomatoes
6

Courgettes
4

Cooked ham
4 slices

Aubergine
1

 Salt, pepper

 : 4–5

Preparation: 15 mins
Cooking time: 30 mins

• Preheat the oven to 200°C.
• Wash all the **vegetables** and slice them thinly, without peeling. Arrange in a large ovenproof dish, interspersed with slices of **ham** cut into quarters and **basil** leaves.
• Season with salt and pepper. Bake for 30 mins and serve.

HEROES' SKEWERS

Chicken legs
4

New red potatoes
4

Limes
2

Red onions
2

Thyme
4 sprigs (fresh or dried)

  Salt, pepper

 Oil

  : 4

Preparation: 10 mins
Cooking time: 45 mins

• Preheat the oven to 180°C.
• Cut 1 **lime** into eight slices, the **potatoes** in half and the **onions** into quarters.
• Assemble 4 skewers, using all the ingredients in turn. Place the skewers in an ovenproof dish and add 2 tablespoons of oil, the juice of the remaining **lime** and the **thyme**. Season with salt and pepper and bake for 45 mins.

SKINNER'S PEAS

Garden peas 400g (fresh or frozen)	Onion 1

Little Gem lettuces 2	Smoked sausages 2

 Salt, pepper

 Oil

: 4

Preparation: 10 mins
Cooking time: 20 mins

• In a casserole dish, sauté the chopped **onion** and the sliced **sausages** with 2 tablespoons of oil for 5 mins. Add the **peas** and the sliced **lettuces**. Cook for 15 mins, stirring occasionally.

• Season with salt and pepper and serve.

PINOCCHIO'S SALTIMBOCCA

Veal escalopes
4 (small and flattened)

Baby spinach
60g

Mozzarella
1 ball

Parma ham
4 thin slices

Rosemary
4 sprigs

 **Salt, pepper**

🐭: 4

🕐
Preparation: 5 mins
Cooking time: 20 mins

• Preheat the oven to 180°C.
• Place the slices of **ham** on the **veal escalopes**. Top with the **baby spinach** and **mozzarella** cut into pieces.
• Roll up and fasten with a sprig of **rosemary**. Place in an ovenproof dish, season with salt and pepper and bake for 20 mins.

PORK WITH PINEAPPLE

Pork chops
4

Pineapple in syrup
2 slices

Soy sauce
8 tablespoons

Coriander
1 bunch (chopped)

 Oil

 : 4

Preparation: 5 mins
Cooking time: 25 mins

• Fry the **pork chops** in a pan with 1 tablespoon of oil for 2 mins. Add the chopped **pineapple**, 6 tablespoons of its syrup and the **soy sauce**. Reduce the heat and cook for 20 mins, basting occasionally with the cooking juices.

• Add the **coriander** and serve.

AGRABAH LAMB WITH POMEGRANATE

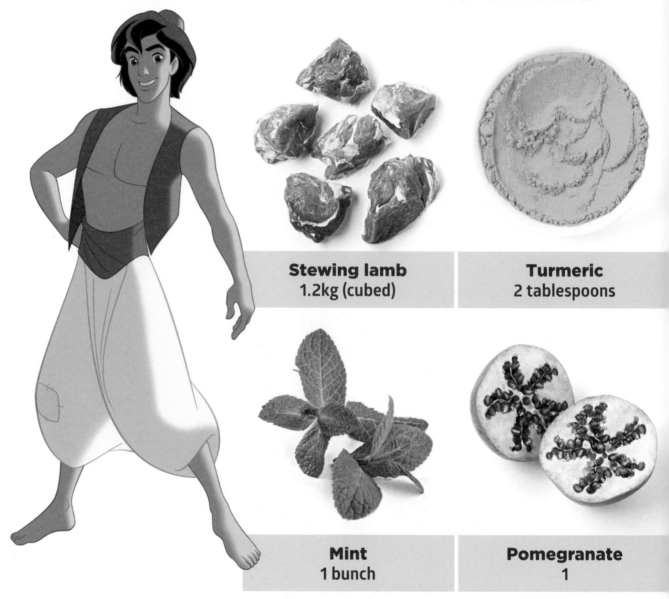

Stewing lamb
1.2kg (cubed)

Turmeric
2 tablespoons

Mint
1 bunch

Pomegranate
1

 Salt, pepper

 Oil

 **: 4**

Preparation: 5 mins
Cooking time: 1½ hours

• In a casserole dish, fry the pieces of **lamb** in 2 tablespoons of oil.

• Add the **turmeric** and 500ml water. Season with salt and pepper and mix. Reduce the heat, cover and simmer for 1½ hours over a low heat.

• Scoop the seeds out of the **pomegranate**, add to the **lamb** and serve with the **mint**.

FAIRIES' CASSEROLE

Lamb shanks
4 (without fat)

Bouquets garnis
2

Garden peas
600g (fresh or frozen)

Mint
1 bunch

 Salt, pepper

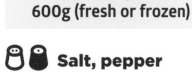 **: 4**

🕐
Preparation: 5 mins
Cooking time: 2 hours

• Preheat the oven to 200°C.

• Place the **lamb shanks** in a casserole dish with the **bouquets garnis** and 500ml water, season with salt and pepper, cover and cook in the oven for 1½ hours.

• Add the **peas** and the **mint** chopped with scissors. Cook for a further 30 mins and serve.

GRANDMOTHER FA'S CHINESE-STYLE PORK

Pork fillet 400g	**Red peppers** 2

Ginger 80g	**Soy sauce** 8 tablespoons	**Roasted cashew nuts** 125g

 Oil

 : 4

🕐

Preparation: 5 mins
Cooking time: 20 mins

• Cut the **pork fillet** into pieces and peel the **peppers** and **ginger**.

• Fry the **meat**, **ginger** and **peppers** lightly in a pan with 1 tablespoon of oil.

• Add the **soy sauce** and **cashew nuts**, then cook for 15 mins over a low heat, stirring occasionally.

ROOT VEGETABLE STEW

Bouquets garnis
2

Rib of beef
1.2kg

Yellow carrots
3

Parsnips
2

Golden Ball turnips
3

 Salt, pepper

 : 4

🕐

Preparation: 10 mins
**Cooking time: 2 hours
45 mins**

• Put the **beef** in a casserole dish, add 2 litres of water, cover and simmer for 2 hours over a low heat.

• Peel the **vegetables** and add them to the casserole dish with the **bouquets garnis**. Season with salt and pepper, cook for a further 45 mins and serve.

CINDERELLA'S STUFFED SQUASH

Red kuri squash
2

Chicken breasts
2

Grated carrot
150g

Grated Parmesan
4 tablespoons

 **Salt, pepper**

🐭 : 4

⏱
Preparation: 10 mins
Cooking time: 40 mins

• Preheat the oven to 180°C.
• Cut the **chicken** into pieces and mix with the **grated carrot** and the **Parmesan**. Season with salt and pepper.
• Cut each **squash** in half, scoop out the contents and stuff with the **chicken** mixture.
• Bake in an ovenproof dish for 40 mins and serve very hot.

THE SNUGGLY DUCKLING'S CASSEROLE

Braising steak
1.2kg

Broad beans
200g (shelled and frozen)

Carrots with stalks
1 bunch

Bouquets garnis
3

  Salt, pepper

 Oil

 : 4

Preparation: 5 mins
Cooking time: 2 hours 40 mins

124

• In a casserole dish, lightly brown the pieces of **beef** with 3 tablespoons of oil for 10 mins. Season with salt and pepper. Add 2 litres of water and the **bouquets garnis**. Cover and simmer for 2 hours over a low heat.

• Add the peeled **carrots** (whole, or chopped if they are large) and the **beans**. Cook over a low heat for a further 30 mins with the lid on.

MOUSSAKA

Aubergines	Minced beef
2	400g (5 % fat)

Tomato passata	Dried oregano	Feta
500ml	2 tablespoons	50g

 Salt, pepper

Olive oil

 : 4

Preparation: 5 mins
Cooking time: 45 mins

- Preheat the oven to 180°C.
- Cut the **aubergines** into pieces and mix in an ovenproof dish with the **minced beef**, **tomato passata** and **oregano**. Season with salt and pepper and sprinkle with crumbled **feta**.
- Bake in the oven for 45 mins and serve with a drizzle of olive oil.

PONGO'S MEATBALLS

Minced beef 600g (5% fat)	Grated Cheddar 80g

Chopped tomatoes 1 small tin (400g)	Dried oregano 1 tablespoon

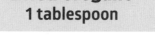 Salt, pepper

Olive oil

: 4

Preparation: 5 mins
Cooking time: approx
25 mins

- Preheat the oven to 200°C.
- Mix the **minced beef** with the **Cheddar** and **oregano** and shape into 8 meatballs. Season with salt and pepper and arrange in an ovenproof dish with the **chopped tomatoes**.
- Bake until the meatballs are cooked through and serve with a drizzle of olive oil.

THE INCREDIBLES' SUPER STEAK

Steaks 4	Broccoli 800g

Olive oil 2 tablespoons	Garlic 4 cloves

  Salt, pepper

☺ : 4

⏱

Preparation: 10 mins
Cooking time: 11 mins

• Cut the **steaks** into pieces and leave until room temperature. Peel and slice the **garlic**. Cut up the **broccoli** and blanch for 5 mins in boiling water.

• A few mins before serving, sauté the **garlic** for 1 min in a pan with the **olive oil**. Add the pieces of **steak** and cook to your liking.

• Add the **broccoli** and cook for 3 mins, stirring continuously. Season and serve immediately.

FLYNN'S QUAILS WITH MUSHROOMS

| Quails 4 | Wild mushrooms 600g |

| Chicken stock 300ml | Bouquets garnis 2 |

 Salt, pepper

 Oil

 : 4

Preparation: 10 mins
Cooking time: 45 mins

• Brown the **quails** lightly in a casserole dish with 2 tablespoons of oil for 10 mins, stirring continuously.

• Pour over the **stock**, add the de-stalked and washed **mushrooms** and **bouquets garnis**.

• Season with salt and pepper, reduce the heat, cover and simmer for 35 mins over a low heat and serve.

TIANA'S JAMBALAYA

Chicken legs
4

Smoked sausages
2

Paprika
2 tablespoons

Rice
400g

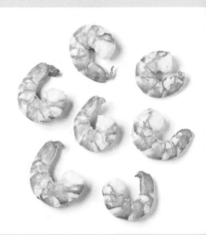

Prawns
200g (cooked and peeled)

 Salt, pepper

☺ : 4

⏱

Preparation: 5 mins
Cooking time: 45 mins

• Preheat the oven to 200°C.
• In an ovenproof dish, mix together the **rice**, **chicken legs**, **prawns**, **smoked sausages** cut into pieces, 1 litre of water and the **paprika**. Season with salt and pepper and mix again.
• Bake for 45 mins and serve.

SNOW WHITE'S CHICKEN IN WHITE SAUCE

Chicken breasts
4

Mushrooms
250g

Tarragon
1 bunch

Greek yogurt
375g

  Salt, pepper

 Oil

 : 4

Preparation: 5 mins
Cooking time: 20 mins

• In a frying pan, sauté the peeled **mushroom** quarters and the **chicken breasts** cut into pieces with 2 tablespoons of oil.

• Cook for 10 mins. Add the **Greek yogurt** and cook for a further 10 mins.

• Season with salt and pepper. Sprinkle with **tarragon** leaves and serve immediately.

WENDY'S CHICKEN

Free-range chicken
1

Broccoli
500g

Romanesco
600g

Pesto
2 tablespoons

Bouquets garnis
2

  **Salt, pepper**

🐭: 5

🕐
Preparation: 15 mins
Cooking time: 50 mins

• Preheat the oven to 180°C.
• Brush the **chicken** with **pesto** and place in a large ovenproof dish. Add the **broccoli** and **romanesco**, cut into pieces, 800ml of water and the **bouquets garnis**. Season with salt and pepper.
• Cook in the oven for 50 mins and serve.

TIMOTHY AND DUMBO'S DELIGHT

Thick steaks 3	Mangetouts 250g

Soy sauce 4 tablespoons	Ginger 50g	Unshelled peanuts 100g

 Salt, pepper

 Oil

 : 4

🕐
Preparation: 5 mins
Cooking time: 5 mins

- Blanch the **mangetouts** in boiling water for 2 mins.
- Peel and grate the **ginger**. Shell the **peanuts**.
- Brown the **meat** cut into pieces with the **ginger** and 2 tablespoons of oil in a frying pan for 2 mins. Add the **mangetouts**, **soy sauce** and **peanuts**, season with salt and pepper, stir and serve.

MERLIN'S PIE

Shortcrust pastry
1 sheet

Sausage meat
250g

Minced beef
250g (5% fat)

Potatoes
400g

Dried thyme
1 tablespoon

 Salt, pepper

 : 4

Preparation: 10 mins
Cooking time: 45 mins

- Preheat the oven to 180°C.
- Peel and dice the **potatoes** and mix with the 2 types of **meat** and **thyme** in a pie dish. Season with salt and pepper and cover with the **pastry**. Trim the edges and seal with a fork.
- Insert 2 small chimneys made out of baking paper and bake for 45 mins. Serve very hot.

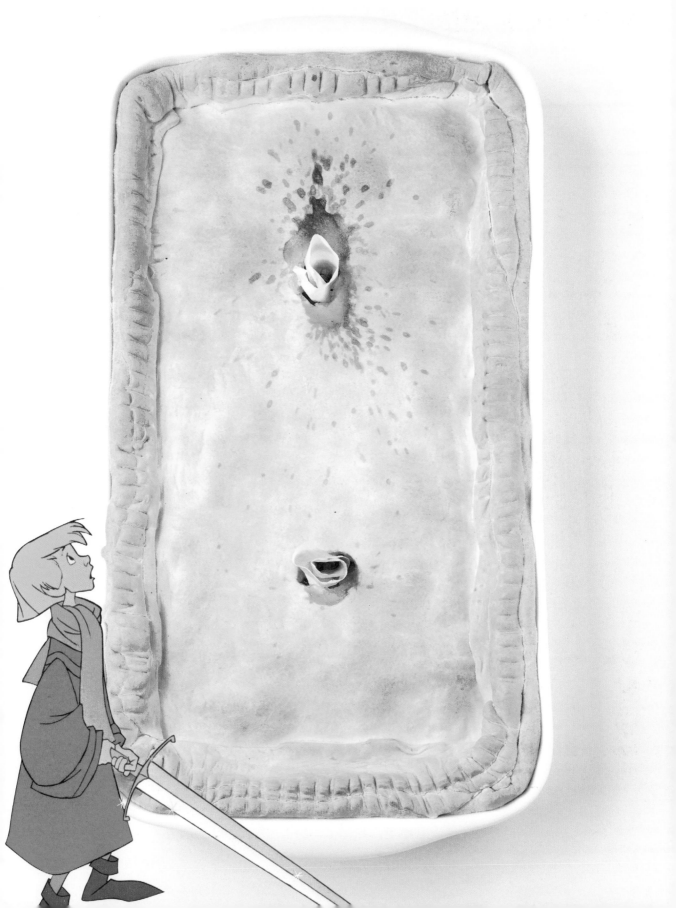

TIANA'S SWEET POTATO CURRY

Stewing pork
1.2kg

Coriander
1 bunch (chopped)

Curry powder
2 tablespoons

Coconut milk
800ml

Sweet potato
1 (about 300g)

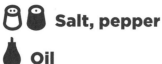 **Salt, pepper**

 Oil

 : 4

Preparation: 5 mins
Cooking time: 2 hours

• In a casserole dish, lightly brown the pieces of **pork** with 2 tablespoons of oil. Add the **coconut milk** and **curry powder**, season then cover and simmer for 1 hour 45 mins over a low heat.

• Add the diced **sweet potato**, cover and cook for 15 mins.

• Serve straight from the dish with **coriander**.

MERIDA'S TROUT

Rainbow trout
4 (whole and gutted)

Flaked almonds
4 tablespoons

Whole hazelnuts
2 tablespoons

Blueberries
2 punnets (125g each)

  Salt, pepper

 Oil

: 4

⏱

Preparation: 5 mins
Cooking time: 25 mins

- Preheat the oven to 180°C.
- Place the **trout** in a large ovenproof dish and add the crushed **almonds** and **hazelnuts**. Season with salt and pepper, drizzle with 2 tablespoons of oil and bake for 15 mins .
- Add the **blueberries**, bake for a further 10 mins and serve.

LASAGNE WITH SMOKED SALMON AND SPINACH

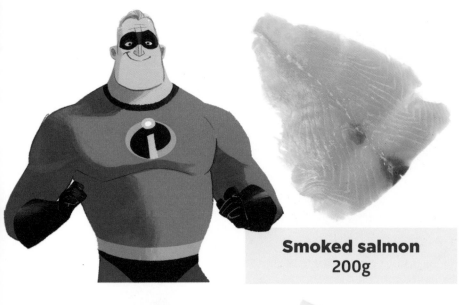

Smoked salmon
200g

Single cream
300ml

Spinach
600g (frozen and thawed)

Lasagne sheets
10

Olive oil
2 tablespoons

 pepper

 **: 4**

Preparation: 20 mins
Cooking time: 30 mins

• Preheat the oven to 180°C.

• In a large bowl, mix the **spinach**, **cream** and **smoked salmon** cut into pieces. Season with pepper. Arrange alternate sheets of **lasagne** and spinach mixture in an ovenproof dish.

• Bake for 30 mins and serve drizzled with the olive oil.

HUEY, DEWEY AND LOUIE'S SKEWERS

Salmon steaks
4 (120g each)

Rosemary
8 sprigs

Courgette
1 (large)

Soy sauce
2 tablespoons

 Salt, pepper

 Olive oil

🐭 : 4

🕐
Preparation: 15 mins
Cooking time: 10 mins

• Preheat the oven to 180°C.
• Cut the **courgette** into broad strips with a paring knife. Cut the **salmon steaks** into 4 pieces and wrap in the **courgette** strips.
• Assemble 8 skewers on the **rosemary** sprigs. Season with salt and pepper. Bake the skewers in the oven for 10 mins and serve with the **soy sauce** and a drizzle of olive oil.

PACHA'S CHILLI

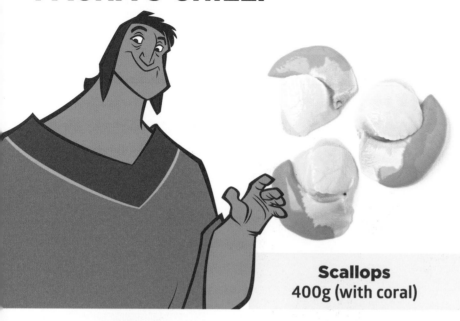

Scallops
400g (with coral)

Red kidney beans
1 tin (800g)

Peeled tomatoes
1 tin (400g)

Ground cumin
2 tablespoons

 Salt, pepper

 Oil

 : 4

Preparation: 5 mins
Cooking time: 20 mins

- Sauté the **scallops** in a casserole dish with 1 tablespoon of oil for 5 mins over a high heat.
- Add the **peeled tomatoes** with their juice, the **cumin** and the **red kidney beans**. Season with salt and pepper.
- Reduce the heat and cook for 15 mins over a low heat, stirring occasionally, and serve.

SALMON FROM HUNDRED-ACRE WOOD

Salmon steaks
4

Crunchy muesli
2 tablespoons (no added sugar)

Unsweetened cranberries
2 tablespoons

Liquid honey
1 tablespoon

Lemons
2

🧂🧂 **Salt, pepper**

: 4

⏱

Preparation: 5 mins
Cooking time: 20 mins

- Preheat the oven to 180°C.
- Place the **salmon steaks** in an ovenproof dish and cover with the **muesli**. Warm the **honey** with the juice of the **lemons** and pour over the **salmon steaks**. Season with salt and pepper and add the **cranberries**.
- Bake in the oven for 20 mins and serve.

FIGARO'S COD

Tomato
1

Cod fillets
2 (about 1kg)

Wholegrain mustard
2 tablespoons

Single cream
200ml

Tarragon
1 bunch

   Salt, pepper

Olive oil

: 4–5

Preparation: 5 mins
Cooking time: 15 mins

- Preheat the oven to 200°C.
- Cut the **cod fillets** into pieces and arrange in an ovenproof dish with the diced **tomato** and the leaves of half the **tarragon**. Mix the **mustard** with the **cream** and 1 tablespoon of olive oil, and spread over the **fish**. Season with salt and pepper bake for 15 mins.
- Add the remaining **tarragon** leaves and serve.

CHIRASHI SESAME SALMON

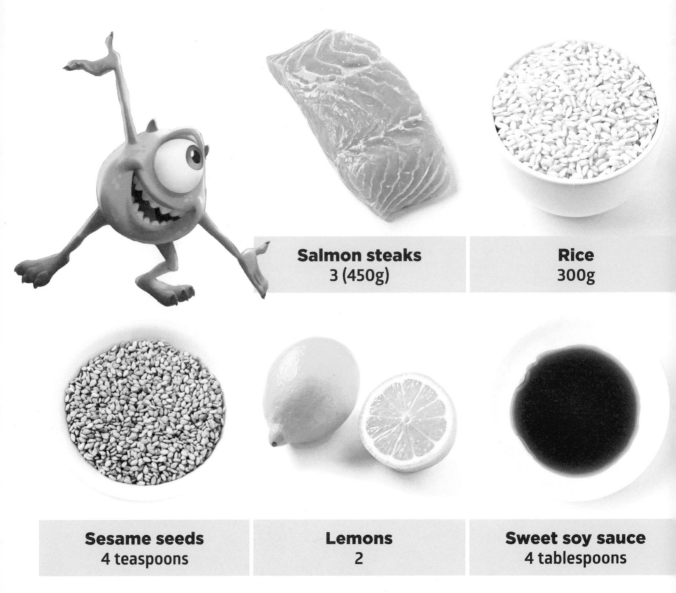

Salmon steaks 3 (450g)	**Rice** 300g

Sesame seeds 4 teaspoons	**Lemons** 2	**Sweet soy sauce** 4 tablespoons

 : 4

🕐
Preparation: 5 mins
Cooking time: 20 mins
Marination: 5 mins

• Put the **rice** in a large bowl with twice the volume of water. Cover with cling film and cook for 20 mins in an 800 W microwave.

• Cut the **salmon** into small pieces and mix with the juice of the **lemons**, the **sweet soy sauce** and the **sesame seeds**.

• Marinate for 5 mins and serve with the **rice**.

DAVID'S COCONUT AND BASIL FISH

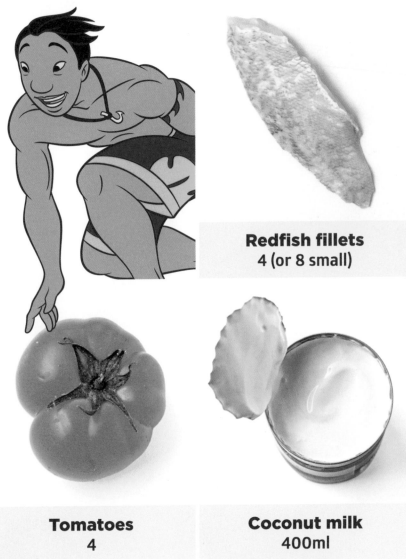

Redfish fillets
4 (or 8 small)

Basil
1 bunch

Tomatoes
4

Coconut milk
400ml

  Salt, pepper

 Olive oil

 : 4

Preparation: 5 mins
Cooking time: 20 mins

- Preheat the oven to 200°C.
- Mix the **coconut milk** with the **basil** leaves and the **tomatoes** cut into pieces. Arrange the **redfish fillets** in an ovenproof dish and pour over the mixture.
- Season with salt and pepper bake for 20 mins.
- Serve with a drizzle of olive oil.

THE SUSHI CHEF'S SPECIALITY

Sushi rice
300g (or risotto rice)

Red tuna
400g

Seasoning
Soy sauce, crystallised
ginger and wasabi

Icing sugar
1 tablespoon

Rice vinegar
6 tablespoons
(or cider vinegar)

🧂 **Salt**

🐭 **: 4**

⏱

Preparation: 15 mins
Cooking time: 10 mins
Resting time: 15 mins

• Wash the **rice** thoroughly. Place in a saucepan with 300ml water, cover and cook for 10 mins over a low heat. Leave to rest for 15 mins.

• Dissolve the **sugar** in the **vinegar**, pour over the **rice**, season with salt and stir until completely cold. Form small sausages of **rice**, top with slices of raw **tuna** and serve with the Japanese **seasoning**.

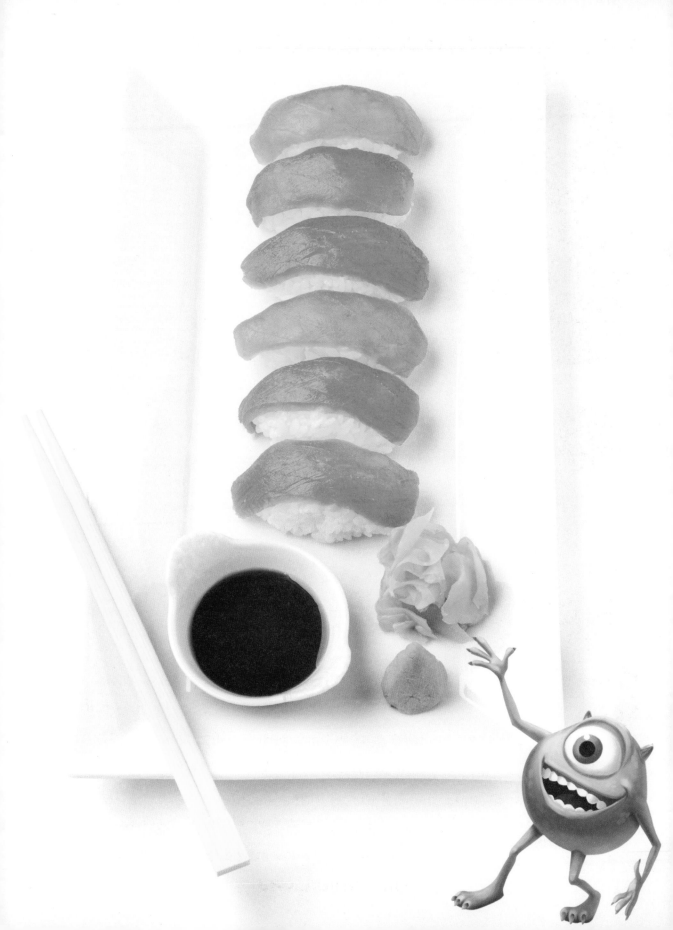

SUPER FITNESS JUICE

| Baby spinach 150g | Pear 1 |
| Orange 1 | Grapefruit 1 | Bananas 2 |

 : 4

Preparation: 5 mins

- Cut 1 slice of **orange** for decoration.
- Chop the **baby spinach**, **bananas** and **pear** into pieces and mix in a blender with the juice of the **orange** and **grapefruit**.
- Pour into glasses. Decorate with the pieces of **orange** and serve immediately.

TEATIME SCONES

Plain flour
250g

Butter
40g (soft)

Milk
150ml

Brown sugar
1 tablespoon

Baking powder
2½ teaspoons

 : 4

Preparation: 15 mins
Cooking time: 12 mins

- Preheat the oven to 220°C.
- Mix the **flour**, **baking powder** and **brown sugar** in a large bowl. Knead with one hand while gradually adding the soft **butter** and the **milk**.
- Form balls of dough and arrange on a baking sheet lined with baking paper.
- Bake for 12 mins and serve warm.

DASH'S CEREAL BARS

Crunchy muesli 100g (no added sugar)	**Dried apricots** 5

Mixed nuts & dried fruit 100g	**Butter** 30g	**Honey** 75g

 : 4

Preparation: 15 mins
Cooking time: 20 mins

- Preheat the oven to 180°C.
- Melt the **butter** and **honey** in a saucepan and pour over the **muesli**, the finely chopped **apricots** and the **mixed nuts and dried fruit**.
- Transfer the mixture to individual traybake tins and bake for 20 mins .
- Leave to cool, turn out and enjoy.

MINNIE'S PALMIERS

Puff pastry
1 sheet

Brown sugar
2 tablespoons

 : 4–5

Preparation: 5 mins
Cooking time: 25 mins
Freezing time: 30 mins

• Preheat the oven to 180°C.

• Unroll the **puff pastry** with its baking paper. Sprinkle with the **brown sugar**.

• Roll each side of the **pastry** tightly towards the centre to form the palmiers.

• Place in the freezer for 30 mins to firm up. Cut into thin slices and arrange on a baking sheet lined with baking paper. Bake for 25 mins.

OLAF'S SNOWBALLS

Desiccated coconut
125g

Sweetened condensed milk
200g

Hazelnuts
20

 : 4

🕐

Preparation: 15 mins
Refrigeration : 3 hours

• Mix 100g of the **desiccated coconut** with the **sweetened condensed milk**. Refrigerate for 3 hours.

• Form 20 balls of the mixture with 1 hazelnut at the centre and coat with the remaining **desiccated coconut**.

CHIP 'N' DALE'S BISCOTTI

Hazelnuts
200g

Plain flour
300g

Baking powder
1¼ teaspoons

Eggs
3

Brown sugar
100g

 Salt

 : 6–8

🕐
Preparation: 10 mins
Cooking time: 20 mins

• Preheat the oven to 180°C.
• Mix together the **brown sugar**, **eggs**, **flour**, **baking powder**, **hazelnuts** and a pinch of salt.
• Form the dough into small logs about 3cm wide and bake for 20 mins on a baking sheet lined with baking paper.
• Cut in 1.5cm slices as soon as they come out of the oven and leave to cool.

RILEY'S POPCORN TREATS

Apples 4	**Greek yogurt** 500g

Cinnamon 1 tablespoon	**Popping corn** 2 tablespoons	**Raisins** 3 large tablespoons

 : 4

Preparation: 5 mins
Cooking time: 11 mins

• Put the **corn** into a large bowl. Cover with pierced microwavable cling film and pop for 3 min in the microwave.

• Mix the diced **apples** in a bowl with the **raisins** and **cinnamon**. Cover and cook for 8 mins in the microwave. Arrange the **apples**, **raisins**, **yogurt** and **popcorn** in glasses and serve.

POOH'S MADELEINES

Butter
100g

Plain flour
120g

Honey
70g

Eggs
2

Baking powder
½ teaspoon

 : 4–5

Preparation: 10 mins
Cooking time: 15 mins

- Preheat the oven to 180°C.
- Grease the madeleine pans and melt the remaining **butter** in the microwave.
- Beat the **eggs** with the **honey** for 1 min with an electric whisk. Add the **flour** mixed with the **baking powder** and the melted **butter**.
- Spoon the mixture into the tins and bake for 15 mins.

NICK'S ICE LOLLIES

Yogurt	Raspberries
4 small pots	1 punnet (125g)

 : 4

Preparation: 5 mins
Freezing time: 2 hours

• Drain the **yogurt** (keeping the pots) and mix with the crushed **raspberries**.

• Spoon the mixture into the empty pots. Insert a wooden skewer in each one and freeze for 2 hours.

• Remove the lollies by breaking the pots with the point of a knife and enjoy.

MOWGLI'S BANANA AND MANGO MOUSSE

Bananas 2	Mango 1

Egg whites 2	Lemon 1

 : 4

Preparation: 15 mins
Refrigeration: 20 mins

- Peel the **bananas** and set 4 slices aside. Purée the remainder of the **bananas** with the peeled and diced **mango** and the juice and zest of the **lemon**.
- Beat the **egg whites** until stiff and then fold in the fruit purée. Spoon the mousse into cups and top with a slice of **banana**.
- Refrigerate for 20 mins and serve.

THE SEVEN DWARFS' BAKED APPLES

Red apples
8

Blackberries
2 punnets (250g)

Honey
2 tablespoons

 : 4

Preparation: 5 mins
Cooking time: 35 mins

- Preheat the oven to 200°C.
- Cut lids off the **apples** and remove the cores. Bake for 25 mins.
- Fill the cooked apples with the **blackberries**, and **honey**, replace the lids and bake for a further 10 mins.
- Serve hot or cold.

184

BALOO'S SKEWERS

Mini bananas
4

Kiwis
2

Desiccated coconut
2 tablespoons

Coconut milk
200ml

Passion fruits
2

 : 4

Preparation: 10 mins

• Peel the **bananas** and **kiwis** and cut into piece
• Assemble 4 skewers with the pieces of **fruit** and sprinkle with **desiccated coconut**.
• Serve with the **coconut milk** mixed with the **passion fruit** flesh.

JASMINE'S ORANGE SALAD

Oranges
5

Blanched pistachios
2 tablespoons

Mint
1 bunch

Orange flower water
4 tablespoons

Honey
1 tablespoon

 : 4

Preparation: 15 mins

• Remove the peel and pith of 4 **oranges** with a very sharp knife. Slice the **oranges** and arrange in a serving dish.

• Add the crushed **pistachios**, **mint** leaves, the juice of the last **orange**, the **orange flower water** and **honey**.

• Serve chilled.

RAFIKI'S BANANAS

Bananas
2

Maple syrup
4 tablespoons

Limes
2

 : 4

Preparation: 5 mins
Cooking time: 10 mins

- Preheat the oven grill.
- Cut the **bananas** in half lengthways, leaving the skins on, and arrange in an ovenproof dish.
- Mix the juice and zest of the **limes** with the **maple syrup** and pour the mixture over the **bananas**.
- Bake for 10 mins and serve hot or cold.

VAIANA'S EXOTIC FRUIT SALAD

Pineapple
1

Passion fruits
2

Mango
1

Star fruit
1 (sliced)

Coconut milk
50ml

 : 4

Preparation: 10 mins

• Cut the **pineapple** in half lengthways, scoop out the flesh and cut into small pieces. Peel and dice the **mango**. Scoop out the flesh of the **passion fruits** and mix with the **coconut milk**
• Mix all the ingredients in the **pineapple** shells, add the **star fruit** and serve chilled.

HARRIS, HUBERT AND HAMISH'S PUDDING

Berries
400g

Ground almonds
125g

Butter
200g (soft)

Brown sugar
125g

Plain flour
125g

Icing sugar

 : 8

Preparation: 10 mins
Cooking time: 30 mins

• Preheat the oven to 200°C.

• Mix the **flour**, **butter**, **brown sugar** and **ground almonds** to a smooth dough. Add the **berries** and mix.

• Transfer the mixture to a rectangular cake tin lined with baking paper. Press down and bake for 30 mins.

• Leave to cool and dust with **icing sugar**.

194

SNOW WHITE'S PLUM TART

Puff pastry
1 sheet

Plums
8

Flaked almonds
125g

 : 4

Preparation: 10 mins
Cooking time: 30 mins

- Preheat the oven to 200°C.
- Stone the **plums** and cut into pieces.
- Unroll the **pastry** on baking paper and press into a tart tin. Spread with the **plums** and 100g of the **almonds**. Fold over the edges. Sprinkle with the remaining **almonds**.
- Bake for 30 mins and serve.

THE MAD HATTER'S PIE

Shortcrust pastry
1 sheet

Rhubarb
400g

Strawberries
250g

Brown sugar
2 tablespoons

 : 4

Preparation: 5 mins
Cooking time: 25 mins

- Preheat the oven to 180°C.
- In a saucepan, cook the trimmed **rhubarb** and **strawberries** cut into pieces with the **brown sugar** for 10 mins over a low heat.
- Spoon the fruit into individual dishes, top with strips of **shortcrust pastry** and bake for 15 mins.
- Serve warm or cold.

AURORA'S BERRY CRUMBLE

| Plain flour 100g | Butter 100g (soft) |

| Brown sugar 100g | Berries 450g (fresh or frozen) |

 : 4

Preparation: 5 mins
Cooking time: 30 mins

- Preheat the oven to 180°C.
- With your fingertips, mix the **butter**, **flour** and **brown sugar** to a crumble dough.
- Cover the base of an ovenproof dish with 350g of the **berries**. Add the crumble and then the remaining **berries**. Bake for 30 mins and serve.

MOTHER RABBIT'S BREAD PUDDING

Stale bread
250g

Eggs
4

Honey
6 tablespoons

Milk
500ml

Raisins
70g

 Butter

 : 6

Preparation: 5 mins
Waiting time: 15 mins
Cooking time: 30 mins

- Preheat the oven to 180°C.
- Beat the **eggs**, then add the **milk** and 5 tablespoons of the **honey**. Add the **stale bread** into small pieces and the **raisins**. Leave to soak for 15 mins.
- Transfer to a greased cake tin and bake for 30 mins. Turn out and serve in thick slices with the remaining **honey**.

RUSSELL'S CRUNCHY MOUSSE

Dark chocolate
200g

Eggs
3

Crunchy muesli
3 tablespoons (no added sugar)

Honey
2 tablespoons

 : 6

Preparation: 15 mins
Refrigeration: 2 hours
Cooking time: 10 mins

• Melt the **chocolate** and mix with the **egg yolks**. Beat the **whites** until stiff and fold into the melted **chocolate**. Spoon into ramekins and refrigerate to set for 2 hours.

• Preheat the oven to 180°C. Bake the **muesli** mixed with the **honey** for 10 mins on a baking sheet lined with baking paper. Leave to cool, crush and sprinkle over the mousses.

EDGAR'S VANILLA CREAM

Vanilla pods
3

Eggs
8

Milk
800ml

Brown sugar
150g

 : 6

Preparation: 5 mins
Cooking time: 40 mins
Refrigeration: 3 hours

• Preheat the oven to 160°C.
• Scrape out the contents of the **vanilla pods**. Beat the **eggs** with the **brown sugar**, add the **milk**, **vanilla** seeds and the **pods** cut into pieces. Mix, transfer to an ovenproof dish and bake for 40 mins in a bain-marie (inside a larger dish filled with water).
• Refrigerate for 3 hours and serve.

CONTENTS

CONTENTS

INDEX OF RECIPES BY INGREDIENT

C

213

INDEX

INDEX

INDEX

NOTES

NOTES

NOTES